SAWYER, KID LAWY[ER]

TEACHER vs. NAPTIME

Written By:
Shanene Muldrow

Illustrated By:
Sheldon Muldrow

For Publishing Information, contact Journal Joy at:
Info@thejournaljoy.com
www.thejournaljoy.com

Paperback ISBN: 978-1-957751-66-5
Hardcover: 978-1-957751-67-2
Ebook ISBN: 978-1-957751-68-9
Editor: Khalia Kai Murray
First edition, 2023

Dedicated to Mom and Dad;
as they always encouraged our creativity and dreams!

"Wake Up Sweetie, Wake Up. It's time for school and you need to eat **breakfast** before you leave."

"I'm up and coming mom. I'm still getting dressed."

Parents laugh – "Oh honey, you will be fine. You barely took a nap all summer. Now let's go before we are late."

"Let's go find your teacher and meet your classmates", Mom said.
"Mrs. Evans, this is Scout and he is here to start his first day. "

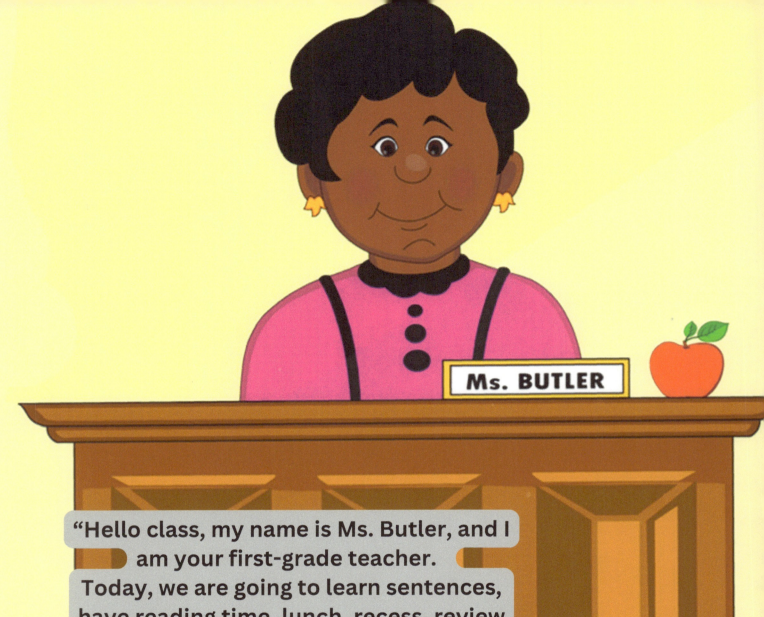

"Hello class, my name is Ms. Butler, and I am your first-grade teacher.
Today, we are going to learn sentences, have reading time, lunch, recess, review our numbers, letters, and then we will have dismissal."

"Class let's pair up and review sentences.
Sawyer, your partner is Rose.
Gavin, your partner is Daniel.
Philip, your partner is Ryan.
Jason, your partner is Isabel.
Natasha, your partner is Eddie."

"Hi Rose, I'm Sawyer. Do you want to know a trick?"

"Yes!, said Rose."
"My parents taught me that if you trace the letter in a color and sound out the word, you will be able to say and read the word."

"I'm tired now and we have to go to recess," Gavin states.

"I will talk to Ms. Butler after recess."

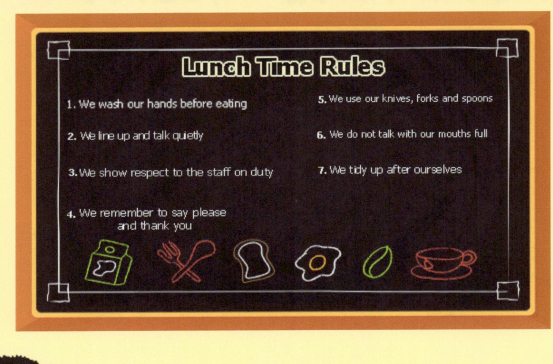

Lunch Time Rules

1. We wash our hands before eating

2. We line up and talk quietly

3. We show respect to the staff on duty

4. We remember to say please and thank you

5. We use our knives, forks and spoons

6. We do not talk with our mouths full

7. We tidy up after ourselves

"I think we need to show Ms. Butler why we need naptime. Eddie, do you have any ideas?"

"No", Eddie replies.

"Hmm, I have an idea. We have to get really tired before recess ends. Let's jump rope, I have one."

Everyone says ok and they share the jump rope.

We need naptime", Sawyer states.
"Why?"
"During recess, we play, run, and jump rope.
Then, we come back inside, and we are very tired."

"The point of recess is to give you a break
from your lesson and exercise.
Sounds like you and your classmates
exercised."

"Ok class, I hear you, and Sawyer gave good points. I will allow 20 minutes after recess to rest your heads on your desk."

The classroom celebrates.

The Creators of Sawyer, Kid Lawyer

Shanene E. Muldrow is the author behind Sawyer, Kid Lawyer. This series is loosely based on her childhood and experiences growing up in Teaneck, New Jersey. In her professional life, she drives effectiveness and efficiency, through project management and communications.

During her downtime, she uses her creativity to develop celebratory experiences for her family and friends and jots down new story ideas for this series.

She is available for speaking engagements and may be contacted via email: at Sawyerkidlawyer@gmail.com.

Website: https://sawyerkidlawyer.com

Shanene E. Muldrow, Author

The Creators of Sawyer, Kid Lawyer

Sheldon B. Muldrow, Shanene's older brother, graduated from Temple University with a Bachelor of Arts in Biology and Fine Arts minor in 2003. Later obtaining his doctorate in podiatric medicine in 2010. While maintaining a career as a healthcare provider, he continues to follow his interests in the arts. He spends some of his spare time drawing in a sketchbook and painting still life.

Sheldon enjoys quality time with family, as much as possible, and is an avid sports fanatic.

Website: https://sawyerkidlawyer.com

Sheldon B. Muldrow, Illustrator

Printed in the USA
CPSIA information can be obtained
at www.ICGtesting.com
LVHW061739110124
768773LV00002B/15